Winston Churchill

The amazing life and legacy of Winston Churchill

Table of Contents

Introduction

Thank you for taking the time to pick up this book about Winston Churchill.

This book aims to serve as a biography of the great Winston Churchill, documenting the key moments in his career and life.

In the following chapters, you will learn about Churchill's early life, his time at war, his time as the Prime Minister, and of course his life after retirement.

Winston Churchill played an instrumental role in history, and will be forever remembered for his courageous leading style and powerful speeches. His role in defeating Nazi Germany is perhaps his greatest achievement, but as you will soon discover, he accomplished much more in his storied life.

Once again, thanks for choosing this book. I hope you enjoy discovering more about the incredible man and leader that was Winston Churchill.

Chapter 1: A Prime Minister is Born

Lord and Lady Randolph Churchill gave birth to their son, Winston Leonard Spencer-Churchill at the Blenheim Palace, Oxfordshire, the United Kingdom. Winston was born on November 30th, 1874 two months before his due date. The Churchills were well known in the aristocratic circles of Oxfordshire, England.

Winston's mother, Jennie Jerome, was an heiress from the United States. She was born in Brooklyn, New York and was the daughter of a wealthy financier. His father, being a British aristocrat, was the third son of Duke number seven of Marlborough. Winston also had a brother by the name of Jack, who was born six years after him. Jennie and Lord Randolph apparently did not have a good relationship, as she was frequently absent in the marriage. Jennie did, however, stay in England after Lord Randolph's death in 1895, and married two more times. Both times she married after Lord Randolph's death, she married men who were twenty years younger than herself.

As a young child, Winston was neglected by his mother and father, and built a strong bond with his nanny, Mrs. Everest. She tried to teach him basic subjects, such as reading, arithmetic, and writing, but he often wouldn't pay attention and usually gave her a hard time. As a young boy, and well into his adulthood, inclusive of his political career, he had a noticeable speech impediment, which he struggled with for years.

Winston was a rambunctious, independent, and rebellious boy. During the early years of his childhood, he spent a lot of time in Dublin, Ireland. When he lived there, his grandfather was Viceroy, with his dad serving as the private secretary of the

Viceroy. With his politically inclined role-models, it is no wonder that Winston entered the political arena in later years.

When he was old enough, Winston attended St. George's School in Ascot, Berkshire, Brunswick School in Hove, and the Harrow School. His military career began at the Harrow School when he joined the Harrow Rifle Corps. While he was away at school, he sent countless letters home to his mother. He begged her to please come and see him, or to come and get him, and to go back home. He hated it there. She rarely ever came to see him, and surely never came and took him with her to their estate.

As far as attending school, Winston was intelligent, but yet he had a downfall. That downfall was that he only cared for particular subjects. They were geography and history, which he excelled at. But with other topics, like Latin and math, they held no interest, and he put forth no effort whatsoever. Because of his lack of drive and bad grades, his father became furious, and this set his father and Winston even further apart.

When he was almost eight years old, Winston was sent off to boarding school; which was the norm for aristocratic families during that time. When he got to the boarding school, he ran into a severe shock, when he found out how forbidding and hostile everyone that worked there acted. He could hardly believe what had happened to his life.

He was so lonely and unhappy. The lonelier he got, the more trouble he caused, and the moodier Winston became. Winston felt like the school was being cruel, hostile, and vile to him, and he did not want to be a part of it. His health started to deteriorate quickly, so much in fact that the family doctor, after examining him, advised he should be removed from the boarding school.

Winston was sent to another school located in a seaside town of Brighton and run by two sisters. They were sympathetic, kind, and the school was a lot smaller and not as pretentious. The cost was also much less. During the three years he was there, Winston almost died of double pneumonia, but he did gradually regain his health and enjoyed studying and learning the subjects that interested him.

When Winston turned twelve, he had his first exams. It was unfortunate for him that the examiners were not so accommodating, and picked out subjects he did not like and this resulted in poor grades. His attempt at gaining entrance to Harrow turned out to be a disaster. After he wrote his name and put a few blotches on his paper, all he could do was stare at it because he did not know one thing about Latin. We will never know if the name Spencer Churchill had anything to do with it, but he was somehow admitted. Much to his father's disgust, Winston entered the lowest class he possibly could at Harrow, and stayed in that same class three times as long as any other boy.

But there were some advantages to this. He bypassed Greek and Latin and took triple studies in English, and that enabled him to earn a living when he reached adulthood. When other guys failed their preliminary tests for the army, Winston passed. One of the tests required him to draw a map of a chosen country. Since he was interested in geography, Winston chose New Zealand, and this was an easy task for him. For the first time, he got a high grade on a test.

When he tried to get into Sandhurst, things were not quite so easy. Sandhurst was the British Army's Military Academy. After he had failed a second time, he left Harrow and went to Captain James and his partners who specialized in cramming skills for assisting students in prepping and getting into the army.

The exam had three requirements: English, Latin, and math, plus two options. Winston chose chemistry and French.

During winter holidays, Winston went to his Aunt, Lady Wimborne's estate. The estate was located in Bournemouth, and he always went there with his twelve-year-old brother Jack, and his mother.

One afternoon while they were there, Jack and their cousin decided they would chase Winston into the estate's fifty-acre pine forest. After a while, Winston got tired and saw a bridge in the distance over a steep cleft. He was sure at this point he had found his escape, but once he reached the middle of the bridge, it dawned on him that his chasers had split up, and they were on either end of the bridge. Winston climbed over the balustrade and jumped off the twenty-nine-foot high bridge aiming for the nearest pine tree. He misjudged the distance between the bridge and the tree and hurled downwards and landed on the hard ground.

Lord Randolph raced immediately from Dublin, went to London, and brought the highest regarded specialists with him. They aimed to take care of Winston, who was badly hurt, and had among all his injuries, a ruptured kidney.

Winston did not regain consciousness for three days, and he was bedridden for three months. His complete recovery took an entire year. During his recovery, he developed a keen interest in politics and national affairs, and went to the House of Commons every chance he got. Because of this, Captain James barely had a chance to prep Winston for his third chance for testing to enter Sandhurst. This time however, he passed with a measure of success; that qualified him for a cavalry cadetship that made Winston very happy.

Young Winston was just an accident waiting to happen it seemed. Later, after he had healed from the ruptured kidney, he almost drowned in a Swiss lake. Winston fell off his horse more times than one can count, and dislocated his shoulder while getting off a steamer ship in India. Churchill crashed a plane while he was learning to fly, and was even hit by a car in New York when he looked the wrong way before he crossed the street on Fifth Avenue.

Once again, however, his father was utterly disappointed and dissatisfied by Winston's lack of exam success. His father wanted him to be joining the 60th Rifles and wrote him a strongly worded letter that stated the same. Winston was shocked at his father's anger, but that was soon forgotten with his delight, to find himself working with horses and spending the last two years of school at Sandhurst.

Winston loved animals his entire life and liked to train horses. He seemed to thoroughly enjoy everything that had to do with Sandhurst. He made a lot of friends while he was there and did not feel so alone. You could see the change, especially during his final exam, as Winston excelled in it. He passed from the Royal Military College of Sandhurst with honors – out of his entire group of 150 cadets, Winston ranked eighth.

Reaching the age of 20 in December of 1894, Winston left the College as an officer of the cavalry in the 4th Hussars. For once, his father seemed proud of him, but he did not live long enough to enjoy it. His father died the next month, January 24th, 1895 after a long illness at the age of 45. His father's long illness is today believed to have been syphilis.

Chapter 2: Winston's Early Career

After Sandhurst, to make some extra money, Winston started writing for newspapers from the wars. He landed a job with the Daily Graphic, and as such he went to Cuba and watched them fighting the Spanish. When his 21st birthday rolled around, to his excitement, Winston came under fire for the first time. During this visit to Cuba is when he tried cigars for the first time and he kept smoking them for the rest of his life. Eventually, Winston Churchill even had a cigar named after him.

During the fall of 1896, he had the chance to fight in India, which was then known as the North-West Frontier. He was sent on a mission scouting up through a valley and became involved in a terrible fight with a tribe. It was there he saw a soldier horrifically slashed to death.

Winston wrote about his experiences during the Siege of Malakand in a book, which was finally published in 1900. He was paid 600 pounds from the publisher, which in today's tender, of course, would have been worth far more.

He soon found himself being sent to Egypt. In 1898, he took part in the Cavalry charge with the British Military at the Battle of Omdurman in Sudan, against Islamic terrorists. At that very time, Winston Churchill told of the dangers of radical Islam. All of a sudden, he found himself as a war correspondent for the newspaper, the Morning Post. The following year, his book, "The River War" about that experience was published. In this book, Churchill told his account of how the British took Sudan and expressed the threat to the Western civilization that radical Islam posed.

Churchill also served as a war correspondent as well as a military officer, which was a dual role that was permitted at the time, in India, South Africa, and the Sudan. When he arrived in South Africa in 1899, his train was ambushed by the Boers, who were descendants of the Dutch settlers that were fighting against the British at the same time. Churchill was taken and marched to a prison camp, but Winston soon escaped by climbing a wall during the night, while two of his fellow prisoners turned and ran back, too frightened to take the chance. Winston had no plan when he escaped, but he stumbled luckily upon a British coal miner's house, who hid him in a mineshaft for three days until they could send him out in a rail truck filled with wool into Mozambique. When he got there, Churchill caught a ship and made his way back to South Africa. Upon reaching the front, he was a hero.

In Churchill's book, the brave and loyal soldiers of the Queen, he states: "The influence of the Islam religion paralyzes the social development of those who follow it. No stronger retrograde force exists in the world. Far from being moribund, Mohammedanism is a militant and proselytizing faith."

"It has already spread throughout Central Africa, raising fearless warriors at every step; and were it not that Christianity is sheltered in the strong arms of science – the science against which it had vainly struggled – the civilization of modern Europe might fall, as fell the civilization of ancient Rome."

Islam, Churchill wrote, "is as dangerous in a man as rabies in a dog."

"How dreadful are the curses which Mohammedanism lays on it votaries! Besides the fanatical frenzy, which is as dangerous in a man as rabies in a dog, there is this fearful fatalistic apathy. The effects are apparent in many countries. Improvident habits, slovenly systems of agriculture, sluggish methods of commerce, and insecurity of property exist wherever the followers of the Prophet rule or live. A degraded sensualism deprives this life of its grace and refinement; the next of its dignity and sanctity. The fact that in Mohammedanism law every woman must belong to some man as his absolute property – either as a child, a wife, or a concubine – must delay the final extinction of slavery until the faith of Islam has ceased to be a great power among men."

In Churchill's 1898 book 'The River' he compares Islam to Christianity:

"Indeed, it is evident that Christianity, however, degraded and distorted by cruelty and intolerance, must always exert a modifying influence on men's passions, and protect them from the more violent forms of fanatical fever, as were protected from smallpox by vaccination. But the Mahommedan religion increases, instead of lessening, the fury of intolerance. It was originally propagated by the sword, and ever since, its votaries have been subject, above the people of all other creeds, to this form of madness."

There were those who claimed that Churchill flirted with Islam after finding a letter written to him by his future sister-in-law when she wrote: "Please do not convert to Islam; I have noticed in your disposition a tendency to orientalise, Pasha-like tendencies, I really have."

One has to wonder if his future sister-in-law ever read any of his books before she wrote this letter.

In 1899, Winston resigned from the Army and had his first taste of politics, as a parliamentary candidate in an election in Oldham, after the sitting MP had died. But unfortunately for Winston, he lost the election.

The Boer War broke out that same year, and once again, Winston was thrown in as the War Correspondent for the Morning Star newspaper. He negotiated a salary of 250 pounds per month, which would be more than 27,000 pounds today. On his way to the Boer War, Winston took with him 60 bottles of 'alcohol.' While he was covering the event, he was taken as a 'prisoner of war,' from the train he was riding on, in South Africa, as the Boers stormed the train. Winston threw himself down in a ditch by the side of the railroad tracks after the train had hit a boulder on the track, that had been intentionally placed there by the Boers for the ambush they had planned. He was found by a Boer soldier, and taken to be locked up in Pretoria. That soldier turned out to be the one and only Louis Botha, who would one day be the Prime Minister of the Union of South Africa. He would, later in life work with Churchill to assist South Africa in becoming a British Dominion.

Winston made a heroic escape and trekked 300 miles to reach safety. But this didn't deter him as he continued to work as a war correspondent. Winston could not stand to sit on the sidelines, and joined the Army again. They commissioned him into the South Africa Light Horse division. Winston took part in the relief of the Siege of Ladysmith, and they took back Pretoria where he had earlier been a prisoner of war.

During his long service in his military career, he had a lot of free time, and spent that time playing some polo as part of a championship team. During this period, he became a self-taught scholar, who had a voracious appetite for all kinds of classic literature and anything to do with the Parliament.

1900 rolled around, he returned to Britain, and his next book was published, 'London to Ladysmith.' In this same year, there was a General Election. Winston Churchill stood as a candidate in Oldham again. This time he won, and his political career began.

In 1904, Winston first met his future wife Clementine at a ball
held at the Earl Crewe residence. The same year, having always
been a part of the Conservative Party, Churchill jumped ship
and joined the Liberal Party. When he left the party, he was
considered a traitor by some of his old Conservative politicians.
Winston disagreed with some of the Conservative policies that
were coming forward, including tariff protection. He also had a
soft spot for improving the welfare of the working class and
desired to help the poor.

In 1908 Winston introduced the Trade Boards Bill, that set up
the first minimum wage ever in Britain. Winston was agreeable
to a referendum to whether women should be allowed to vote.
He supported the People's Budget which saw the growth of the
Welfare State and introduced an income tax to pay for it. This
budget helped the life of the poor and addressed the inequality
in British Society.

During his twenties, Winston Churchill proposed to three
different ladies, all of whom refused him. However, he did
remain good friends with all of them.

In 1908, Winston ran into Clementine Hozier who was attending
the same London dinner party as he. It so happened that they
were seated next to each other. Some say their marriage came
about because Winston needed a wife and she needed a
husband. Winston seemed to be attracted to Clementine because
of her grittiness that was most unusual for women at that time.
Clementine was attracted to Winston because he was a rising
politician from a prominent family in the country, who was
charming, with such a terrific personality.

The day he was to propose to her, he had promised to take her
on a walk around the Blenheim Palace grounds, but then he
overslept. Fortunately, his cousin Charles knew what was going

on and took Clementine for a carriage ride so she wouldn't leave, and sent a servant to make Churchill get out of bed.

He married her less than one month after they had announced their engagement. They married in St. Margaret's Church located in Westminster, London on August 11, 1908.

Their relationship was pretty stormy. Winston and Clementine both had domineering personalities and would not deny themselves of something that they wanted. Winston wanted power, and Clementine wanted to dominate Winston. No matter how much they fought, they loved each other. Neither one of them ever looked outside the marriage for extramarital affairs. The longer they were married, the more they fussed. He was gone a lot during the 1930's and was pretty frustrated. He wanted to wake the country up and rearm the British, and did not seem to be having much luck with it.

 It made him so difficult for Clementine to deal with. During the years of 1940-1945, while Winston had Supreme power, they were closer than at any other time during their marriage.

   To their union were born five children: There was Diana who was born in 1909-and became an actress, who in her adult life suffered several nervous breakdowns. She died in 1963 at age 54 from suicide by a drug overdose.

Then Randolph was born in 1911, and he wanted so badly to be like his father. He was a journalist and also wanted to be Prime Minister one day. Unfortunately, he had such an addiction to alcohol that most people in Britain soon gave him the cold shoulder and no one wanted him around. So, Randolph went to the United States to give speeches, but his money was spent on wine and women. He did marry, but divorced after about six years. He died in 1968 in his home at the age of 57, from a heart attack.

Sarah was born in 1914, and she too was an actress. She was well known for her success. Sarah passed away in 1982 at the age of 68 from an overdose of sleeping pills.

Marigold was born in 1918, and at the age of 2 ½ years, contracted tonsillitis. It developed into septicemia and brought on her death in 1921. Antibiotics were not discovered until WWII when they discovered penicillin. If only there had been penicillin in 1921, Marigold would have probably survived her tonsillitis and would not have become septic. The death of Marigold shook Clementine to the core.

Then there was Mary who was born in 1922, who was the baby of the family, and was conceived during the dark months after Marigold's death. Clementine hired a cousin who was very responsible, known as Nana to take care of the new precious baby. Mary was very close to both of them, and very involved in everything to do with World War II. Mary could remember her Dad's memory as being formidable. He could recite Macaulay, Shakespeare, and Byron forever. She died at age 91 from a stroke on May 31, 2014, as a very wealthy woman with approximately $23 million dollars to her name.

Mary was involved in a lot of charities and other organizations in Britain. She wrote books about her father and her mother, as well as a book about herself as the daughter of Winston Churchill. All were top-rated books. One book covered the love letters that Mary uncovered after the death of her mother, and it was evident that Winston and Clementine loved each other deeply.

At first impression, one might notice that they both came from well-to-do backgrounds, and what may have drawn them to each other was their insecurities from their childhoods. Clementine seemed to provide an emotional blanket and a sounding board politically, which was important in keeping Winston as a dominant politician of his age. Believe me; there was no doubt that he was something for Clemmie to deal with, because at the time he was domineering and self-absorbed.

He was such a handful to cope with: moody, petulant, prone to depressions and when he was not in power and control, he was grumpy.

Winston usually would not take advice from anyone and would almost always browbeat others into submission. However, Clemmie wasn't afraid of him and would argue with conviction and skill. Clementine was insightful and persuasive, but she always kept both her eyes on his political career. It didn't matter if she was shoring up his opinions or stopping him from making himself a fool politically in the Commons. Often making him think of the ordinary people's views; Clementine was the only person who could change Winston's mind.

Because of Clementine's persuasive success with Winston, there was a constant succession of generals and politicians that would come to her if he needed some persuasion or nudging in a different direction. When Winston declared he was going out on the Belfast so he could watch D-Day firsthand, Clemmie had King George VI himself come to her to stop his dangerous scheme.

When the couple argued, it was always Winston who asked for peace, often by one of the hundreds of letters they would send to each other.

In one of their letters Winston had penned he told her, "My darling one, I have been fretting over our interchange … forgive me for anything that seemed disrespectful to you."

In 1909, a woman who was working to get voting rights for women attacked Churchill on a train platform in England by lashing at him with a dog whip. The woman tried to push him in front of a moving train. Clementine leaped over luggage as quick as a flash and dragged Winston by his coat tails from falling in front of the train. During a crisis, there was no one as good to have around as Clemmie.

December 1910 came, and the Jewish Anarchists from Latvia were carrying out a raid on some jewelers on the East End when the police found them. They killed three of the policemen. Two weeks later an informant came forward and tipped the cops off that the two murderers were hiding out in a home on Sidney Street. By the 2nd of January, at early dawn, over 100 police officers had surrounded the street. The criminals had tons of ammo, and the police force came under heavy assault. Winston Churchill at the time was the Home Secretary, and he went down to see what was going on for himself. He gave orders that the Scots Guards were to be brought in to assist the police.

Some accounts tell that a bullet went through Winston's top hat during the shootout. The house the criminals were in finally caught on fire, and the fire department was standing ready to go into the building. But Winston stopped them. Winston later said, "I thought it better to let the house burn down, rather than risk decent British lives in rescuing those worthless rascals."

The criminals inside the house never came out alive.

In 1911, Churchill decided to use some of the naval funds to help develop a tank, something he thought would be useful in the war. He was also very interested in the use of airplanes in combat. Winston was so fascinated with aerial combat that he started taking flying lessons. He never got his license to fly though after he got hurt in a plane crash at Croydrome, and Clementine asked him to give up this new hobby.

In 1913 the Mental Deficiency Act came up, and Winston was in favor of sterilizing the mentally challenged, but, this did not pass. Instead, they were to be put into institutions.

When World War I broke out, Winston was First Lord of the Admiralty, a post he had held since 1911. In this role, he prepared a water assault against the falling Ottoman Empire. Winston thought that such an action would give the British a chance to link up with their allies, the Russians, and put added pressure on Germany's front in the east. The assault was thought to possibly tip the scales on the entire conflict. Allied battleships came through the Dardanelles Strait, which is near what we know today as Istanbul, in March 1915. Firing from the Ottoman sank three of them, damaged three others severely, and the others retreated. Allied troops did not gain any ground during those months of fighting on the Gallipoli Peninsula, and suffered greater than 250,000 casualties. Winston lost his admiralty post because of this failure.

Winston was eager to restore his reputation, so he volunteered to join the Western Front. After spending a short period in the Grenadier Guards he was made a Lt. Colonel in the 6th Battalion.

In 1917 Churchill was assigned the position of Minister of Munitions which had him managing the monies during the war. It took strong skills administratively to be able to do what he did with so little. He was considered to be a skilled and efficient minister.

In 1921 at the Cairo Conference, while Churchill was serving as foreign secretary of colonial affairs, he made if abundantly clear that his views about the dangers of Islam had not changed.

He went on to say, "They hold it as an article of duty, as well as of faith, to kill all who do not share their opinions and to make slaves of their wives and children. Austere, intolerant, well armed, and bloodthirsty," he said of adherents to Islam.

In 1924 Winston was then appointed to be Chancellor of the Exchequer. He took the advice from 'many' economists and returned Britain to the "Gold Standard" at a pre-war level. Instead of helping, it was terribly damaging to the economy, and caused a period of deflation, low growth, and high unemployment. Winston later admitted that this decision was his largest domestic mistake.

The declining living standards did not help, but rather seemed to contribute to the Strike in 1926. Churchill wanted to stop the strikers and put the trade unions out of business. At this time in his life, he admired Mussolini for being such a strong leader.

Chapter 3: Churchill Rises to Power

In 1930's Europe there was a type of peace movement that contributed to a form of political isolation for Mr. Churchill. Most of the British subjects worked to avoid confrontation, and they themselves chose to ignore Hitler's rise to power.

Churchill seemed to have grown weary of Hitler as early as the first part of October 1930. Churchill was quoted as saying that, if Hitler came to power in Germany, England's response would have to be swift. He said, "If a dog makes a dash for my trousers, I will shoot him down before he can bite." It seemed that Churchill had to endure an endless uphill struggle to be heard when he warned of the impending doom of Europe. Until 1932, Adolf Hitler and Winston Churchill had never met. Who knows how it might have changed history in the world if they had, or if the Nazi Hitler had made different decisions in that 1932 spring. Churchill was already standing in the Grand Hotel Continental Munich's lobby. He was unshaven, wearing a shabby trench coat, and exhausted from running his election campaign. In another room, he was dining with his family and other members of his entourage, and they were all waiting for Hitler.

Winston Churchill, the short, stout British man that he was, from one of England's most elite families, was already a famous person. At this point in his life he was already a successful journalist. He had authored bestsellers, and before WWI had served as home secretary president on the Board of Trade, First Lord of the Admiralty (he was head of the navy). During the time of World War I, Winston was appointed as Secretary of State for War, Minister of Munitions as well as Secretary of State for Air. After World War I, Winston became Secretary of State for the Colonies and then he served from 1924 to 1929 as the Chancellor of the Exchequer. The British Isles had never seen anyone like Winston Churchill, with such an illustrious career, in a long time.

Churchill went to Munich to conduct some research for his new book. While there, he wanted to meet the notorious Hitler, whose supporters were actually in the process of destroying the Weimar Republic. Churchill's son, and Hitler's foreign press agent, whose name was Ernst "Putzi" Hanfstaengl arranged for Hitler and Winston to meet over dinner at the Continental Hotel. Even though Hanfstaengl forgot the tell the Churchills that the Fuehrer had shown little interest as to whether he would even show up or not.

The evening continued without Hitler making an appearance. After dessert, Hanfstaegl asked to be excused and hurried to the hotel telephone to call Hitler and ask him if he was going to show up or not. All of a sudden, he saw Hitler standing in the lobby. The Nazi had unexpectedly met with a supporter at the Continental Hotel.

Hanfstaengl took Hitler aside and told him that if Winston Churchill would see him now, that his failure to have shown up for dinner might be seen as an insult. He became quite frank and told Hitler that he needed to go in there, as it was important that he did so. Hitler stood his ground and told Hanfstaengl that he had a lot to do and just did not have the time. Hitler went to bed.

Winston was kind about the rejection. Later that evening, Hanfstaegl went to the piano in the hotel's music room, and they all sang Scottish songs. Churchill wrote in his memoirs that he regretted that Hitler lost his only chance to meet.

One has to wonder if Hitler had met with Winston in Munich that night, would he have realized at that time that he was facing someone who was every bit his match? That he was meeting with a man, who enjoyed war? That he was meeting a man, who would finally bring Hitler to his knees?

Churchill was truly a man who loved danger. It was as simple as that. As a young man, he had killed people in battle, but he was not bothered by the killing experience. He felt that nothing in history was ever settled, except by wars. When he reached his sixties, as prime minister, he would stand on one of the government buildings in London during German air raids so he could watch the murderous scene from above, while all his cabinet ministers would run to the bomb shelters.

Winston Churchill and Adolf Hitler; there was a rivalry that pitted the two men so against each other, unrivaled by anything seen for years. Was it because of the petite want-to-be-world-ruler up against the son-of-the-aristocracy, or was it a puritan against a degenerate. It could also have been a militant against a realist, a murderer against an adventurer, or a racist revolutionary up against an imperial political realist.

The entire world, as to the way it existed in 1938, was showing little comfort for Neville Chamberlain and his policy of appeasement. He seemed to like to put his head in the sand and hope that everything would just go away. The Anschluss of Austria came to be a direct challenge to the British and their sense of national integrity.

It had been eight years since Hitler had failed to show up for dinner at Munich. The duel between Winston Churchill and Hitler was going to shape the fate of the entire world. Manchester does give a glimpse of Winston's hope that maybe Hitler, who was like a boa constrictor that has swallowed an animal whole, would find out that Austria was more than he could handle. Churchill was always ready to take the political advantage and be the ever staunch supporter of firm resolve, and stood ready with a stark criticism of every little move Chamberlain made. To Winston, the realities seen made things very clear. Hitler now had Austria and was poised to take over the Sudentenland, if not all of Czechoslovakia. The British economy was suffering, and struggling to recover from the great Depression, and support for another conflict was just not present.

Chamberlain decided to set out on two trips to meet with Hitler. One of them at Berchtesgaden and another at Godesberg. Chamberlain with a background in business thought he could handle Hitler like any other business negotiation. He was sure if he could determine Hitler's bottom line, and just give it to him, the problem would all be over. When Hitler revealed he wanted the Sudentenland as his territorial request, Chamberlain decided it was a small price to pay for preventing a World War. However, it never once occurred to Chamberlain that Hitler would lie to him, which was what Winston Churchill feared. What Hitler had asked for, he got. Chamberlain was happy about the deal. When the four powers finally met (France, Germany, Britain, and Italy) in Munich, Czechoslovakia's fate was determined. The Munich Conference was merely to figure out how to give Hitler his prize, rather than decide if he deserved it or not.

When Chamberlain returned from Munich and seeing the people roar with exhilaration, Chamberlain was sure that this bargain with Hitler would make sure of his political future. The public was relieved that war was averted, the House seemed content with the status quo, and the rest were the voices of naysayers in the cabinet. Duff Cooper (serving as First Lord of Admiralty), resigned. Churchill had a response that one would expect: "How could honorable men with experience and good records in the Great War condone a policy that is so cowardly? It was sordid, sub-human, suicidal, and squalid… The last sequel to the sacrifice of honor." When he was reviewing the Munich Agreement, Winston announced to the House of Commons, "There can never be absolute certainty that there will be a fight if one side is determined that it will give completely away."

The Munich Conference did not do much to dispel Stalin's feeling that the western powers were colluding against him. Stalin wanted a military and political agreement between France, Britain and the Soviet Union. The time would come when Stalin's patience with the western powers would stop. Stalin was watching his neighborhood shrink right before his eyes and having the Nazi's knocking on his front door was just not going to be acceptable. Munich was the real final blow to any possible alliance. Ambassador Seeds cabled, "I think that we take it that Mr. Molotov will not volunteer any new proposals in the near future." The Soviet's attitude to the Western Powers and their abilities to deal effectively with international crises can best be summed up by Litvinov's last speech to the League of Nations, September 21, 1938: "A fire brigade was set up in the innocent hope that, by some lucky chance, there would be no fires. … every State must define its role and its responsibility before its contemporaries and before history. That is why I must plainly declare here that the Soviet Government will bear no responsibility whatsoever for all the events now taking place, and for the final consequences which ensue."

And proceed they did. After Molotov had taken Litvinov's place and the German diplomatic corps was put into action, it immediately started happening. Hitler, along with France and Britain, had attained a major goal of his foreign policy that day in Munich by isolating the Soviet Union from the diplomatic scene internationally.

The isolation that was gained by France and Britain made them seem to be the ones responsible. It caused a feeling that a non-aggression type of treaty with the Nazis would be the only possible protection for Stalin. Ribbentrop was prepared to use his personal bearing on the Soviet leader, and with enthusiasm, to convince Stalin of what possibilities this opened up for the treaty with Nazi Germany. Stalin was a success, and come August of 1939, the Nazi-Soviet Pact was finalized.

Churchill, on the other hand, had begged the Chamberlain government to try to form an alliance with France and the Soviet Union to deter a German reproachment. Manchester himself suggests that Churchill was the one who proposed the "Grand Alliance", modeled after the one which won the Great War. He felt that the resolute and unified front might cause Hitler to back down. Churchill even thought that this show of force might cause a defection within the German Army once they were challenged with the possibility of war with this type of alliance.

Now that the Germans had their Eastern front settled, they entered Poland on September 1, 1939. Winston realized the government's commitment they had to Poland and knew that they must keep it. War was declared September 3, 1939. It was necessary for Churchill to give a speech to the House of Commons that caused a packed House.

During World War II, there was a clutch of "basement Offices in Whitehall" that served as the epicenter of Britain's war effort. It was known as the "Cabinet War Rooms," and was occupied by heads of the government, including the Ministers, Prime Minister and military strategists.

There had been plans since the 1920's to evacuate the essential staff, cabinet, and Prime Minister if necessary. But they became concerned that Londoners might feel abandoned if all the heads of government were in a safe place. They decided to find an emergency shelter in the middle of London.

In June 1938, they selected the location for the New Public Offices. They made it near Parliament. It was built with a large basement and had a strong steel frame.

The basement was set up to allow for meetings of the War Cabinet to use during the times of air raids, and it also housed an entire military information center. The room became very busy on August 27, 1939, which was a week before Britain announced they were declaring war on Germany.

Churchill's War Group met there 115 times, but most often during the Blitz and then later during the German V-weapon offensive.

May 13, 1940, Churchill made a speech, "You ask: 'What is our policy?' I will say: 'It is to wage war by sea, land, and air, with all our might and with all the strength that God can give us: to wage war against a monstrous tyranny, never surpassed in the dark, lamentable catalog of human crime.'

That is our policy. You ask: 'What is our aim?' I can answer in one word: 'Victory! Victory at all costs, victory in spite of all terror, victory however long and hard the road may be; for without victory there is no survival."

These very rooms were in use 24 hours a day for six years until August 16, 1945. It was the first time that the lights were turned off since they were turned on August 27, 1939.

Just before Christmas 1941, Sir Winston visited the White House. The stay lasted 24 days and was very secretive, but it made quite an impact on the staff of the White House. They had a difficult time adjusting to his 'oddities.' Chief Usher, J.B. West stated "We got used to his 'jumpsuit,' the one-piece uniform he wore every day, but the servants never quite got over seeing him naked in his room when they would go up to serve brandy. He was in his jumpsuit or nothing. In his room, Mr. Churchill wore no clothes at all most of the time during the day."

When the time came that Churchill was to confront the Nazis and their threat to Europe, the people of Britain were there to stand behind him.

Winston's failure at Gallipoli would forever haunt him. Many World War II historians think that was his reason for delaying the invasion of France, until he felt sure that he had an incredibly high chance to succeed. A very emotional Churchill told General Marshall, "I see the sea full of corpses."

For a long time now, Churchill had been that lone voice that spoke to and for the British when Hitler's evil was seeping into the countryside. Churchill's consistent stance and his dogged determination against appeasement gained him credibility with the British folk when he became Prime Minister. Winston had no reason to hate Chamberlain, and Winston didn't. Churchill felt convinced that Chamberlain had been advised inaccurately on some facts, and that if he had been advised more wisely, Chamberlain would have taken a better plan of action.

Churchill usually did not sleep more than five hours each night, plus he took a mid-day nap. He had such a strong constitution that it allowed him to be in constant attendance on the matters of the state well into the late evening and early morning hours.

Sir Winston was a very emotional man. He would frequently break down in sobs even during meetings, when he heard sad news, and even in many of his speeches that broadcast on the radio, you could hear him holding back tears.

During the time of World War II, and despite Churchill's misgivings about communism, he did ally himself with the Soviet's during this time. After the war, he began to have serious doubts about the aims of the Soviet Union. In March 1946 he gave a speech, in which he spoke of "an iron curtain has descended across the continent.

Behind that line, countries are subject to a very high and, in many cases, increasing control from Moscow." From that point on, Western folks continuously mentioned the "iron curtain" when they talked about the USSR.

July 1945 rolled around, and Germany had finally surrendered, but Japan had not. Britain was holding its first general election in a decade. Churchill's party which was Conservative, lost by a landslide. His party was portrayed by the other party, the Labour Party as anti-welfare and anti-worker. Churchill reminded his supporters "They have a right to kick us out. That is a democracy. That is what we have been fighting for." He was re-elected to the post again in 1951 and remained there until ill health caused him to resign three-and-a-half years later.

Clementine usually accompanied Winston to his public events. No matter where they went, he was greeted by ecstatic and large crowds. Light security today is unheard of, but on VE Day, Clementine drove Winston through London in an open car when he went to formally visit Allie's embassies. Being guarded by four mounted police and a few outriders; they passed on streets lined with celebrating and noisy crowds.

Churchill was always very, very moved by people who reacted to him. There would be times he had tears running down his cheeks. When Winston lost the election in 1945, it was Clementine that threw the fit.

In 1953, Churchill received the Nobel Prize Award in Literature for his mastery of biographical and historical description, as well as his brilliant speaking in defending human values.

In June of 1953, Churchill suffered a severe stroke in his office at 10 Downing Street, and he retreated to his country home and did not return to public life until October.

Before the end of his life, Winston turned out to be a very accomplished artist. He had, with the encouragement of one of his friends, Paul Maze, taken up painting during World War I. During his lifetime he had painted over 500 works of art on canvas in oils. Churchill painted mostly landscapes, but some were interior scenes and a few were portraits. He did not do well with retirement and went through periods of great depression.

Very few people know Churchill's connection with Hallmark Cards. Hall's friendship with Churchill began when Hall went to hear Churchill's speech at the Westminster College in Fulton, Missouri, March 5, 1946.

Hall remembered Winston's "firm handshake and his direct eye contact. "Not long after Churchill had been at Fulton, Winston published an essay, 'Painting as a Pastime.' Churchill had never before sold his work; he had always given his paintings away to family and friends. He had only sold one painting, and that had been for charity. Hallmark wanted to use Churchill's paintings on their Christmas cards. They contacted Winston Churchill, and when he heard the Hallmark name, he agreed. He said, "they are a good firm and to make a deal with them and tell them I am delighted at the opportunity of having my paintings exhibited through the medium of Christmas cards."

Churchill invited Hall, his wife, and their son Donald to visit him at Chartwell in the summer of 1950. J.C. remembered Churchill wearing his 'siren suit.'

As they toured the Churchill grounds, they observed Winston's 'maggot moment,' when Churchill flung a handful of maggots to his golden orfe. Winston asked Elizabeth Hall if she would like to feed the orfe. She wasn't squeamish so she held out her hand and he gave her about a dozen maggots so that she could feed the fish.

Hall later wrote that Churchill had such affection for the wild pets and birds and swans on his estate.

Churchill wanted to know from Hall if he was happy with the sales of the cards. J.C. told him they were delighted as they had sold over a million in the first year. Winston's only complaint was that they were flattering his paintings. He went on to express his curiosity about the cards, the distribution, reproduction, shipping, sales and what would happen if the product didn't sell. Hall told Churchill that it was something which he did not have to be worried about, as the cards were selling so well.

At a later time, the "Hallmark Hall of Fame" had an hour long television show about Churchill's 'Painting as Pastime,' and called the show "The Other World of Winston Churchill," and made sure to coincide it with Winston's 90th birthday.

Before Churchill's retirement in 1955 as Prime Minister, he made a speech to the Commons in which he ended with these words: "The day may dawn when fair play, love for one's fellow men, respect for justice and freedom, will enable tormented generations to march forth triumphant from the hideous epoch in which we have to dwell. Meanwhile, never flinch, never weary, never despair."

In February 1956 Winston suffered another minor stroke. Despite his failing health, Churchill's legacy was already one of a hero.

In 1963, U.S. President John F. Kennedy proclaimed Churchill as an Honorary Citizen of the United States. In 2002, Churchill was named the Greatest Britton of all time in a BBC poll, based on about a million votes from BBC viewers.

Chapter 4: Churchill's Thoughts & Speeches

From what one learns about Churchill, one can't help but admire the man. Unfortunately, he was often away from his children, much as his parents were away from him as a child. But he spoke the truth when he did speak, and his words had such depth that they are remembered to this day. Churchill always believed in giving someone a second chance. He sought to understand the plight of others. He never seemed actually to hate anyone. He had some he disliked, but you cannot point to anyone that you could say Churchill hated. He never seemed to harbor hate. This was considered by many to be a great testament to his noble character.

Throughout much of his life, Churchill opposed that India should have any self-government. He had such a dislike for their leader Mohandas Gandhi who was supposedly nonviolent and independent. At one point, Churchill called him a 'disloyal Middle Temple lawyer posing as a fake of the type well known in the East.' He even felt they should let Gandhi die during one of his hunger strikes. Churchill's attitude shone through in other British colonies as well. Winston once said that, for example, that Zulus, Dervishes, and Afghans were nothing but 'barbarous and savage people.'

Winston Churchill took his position as Prime Minister in 1940. This was after a terrible start to World War II, and after Nazi Germany had already conquered most of Europe. Winston was a fantastic public speaker, and he did his best to rally the British in the face of what was a near-certain attack. He gave six major speeches in a four-month timeframe. In one of his first speeches, he told Parliament that "all he had to offer was blood, sweat, tears, and toil." Then on June 4, he declared "We shall defend our island, whatever the cost may be. We shall fight on the beaches; we shall fight on the landing grounds, we shall fight in the fields and the streets, we shall fight in the hills. We shall never surrender." On June 18, as France was preparing to submit to the Nazis, he told his countrymen to "brace ourselves to duties and so bear ourselves that if the British Empire and its Commonwealth last for a thousand years, men will still say, "This was their finest hour."

Winston Churchill had some bits of wisdom to share about life and love as well:

"My most brilliant achievement was my ability to be able to persuade my wife to marry me."

"To improve is to change; to be perfect is to change often."

"Immature love says, I love you because I need you, Mature love says, I need you because I love you."

"My wife and I tried to breakfast together, but we had to stop, or our marriage would have been a wreck."

"We make a living by what we get, but we make a life by what we give."

"If you are going through hell, keep going."

"If you have an important point to make, don't try to be subtle or clever. Use a pile driver. Hit the point once. Then come back and hit it again. Then, hit it a third time – a tremendous whack."

"Courage is what it takes to stand up and speak; courage is also what it takes to sit down and listen."

"Time passes swiftly, but is it not joyous to see how great and growing is the treasure we have gathered together."

"Success is not final; failure is not fatal: it is the courage to continue that counts."

 "Courage is going from failure to failure without losing enthusiasm."

Winston Churchill's life taught us that our journey through life would not be complete if we did not fail now and then, as we all become better at it. In the society that we live in now, it seems that failure needs to be avoided. It is supposedly embarrassment at its finest, and we all feel a sense of humiliation publicly when failure happens. This way of thinking is flawed.

Churchill had bipolar depression, a rather debilitating mental illness. In hindsight, this mental illness may have been what drove him to his full potential and his greatness. It is when we fail that our weaknesses and failures will burst forth.

It seemed that maybe Churchill's greatest challenge might have been his depression that kept haunting him. It was enough that he was not silent about it. He called it his "Black Dog." The Churchill family seemed to suffer from this same type of depression. Winston, just like his father, suffered from severe mood swings. Lord Beaverbrook said that Winston was "always at the top of the wheel of confidence or the bottom of the intense depression." Churchill's neurologist felt he had cyclothymia which is a mood disorder that is similar to bipolar disorder, but not as severe.

Unfortunately, those who do suffer from Bipolar Disorder have periods of Mania, when they may get no sleep whatsoever, and they remain on top of their game.

But, when they do not have anything to keep them always stimulated, they usually go to the bottom of the spiral and sink back into a deep depression.

Some of his teachers felt he suffered from what is known today as Attention Deficit Hyperactivity Disorder. Others, however, thought that he only applied himself to subjects that he liked; when all along it may have been the beginnings of bipolar disorder. No matter which it was, his 'disorder' seemed to serve him quite well as a leader.

Winston Churchill once defined tact as "the ability to tell someone to go to hell in such a way that they look forward to the trip."

Winston Churchill was known for his incredible dry humor and wit. He is credited with more than one exchange, but a couple I will include here.

An exchange with Bessie Braddock: "Winston, you are drunk, and what's more, you are disgustingly drunk"; "Bessie, my dear, you are ugly, and what's more, you are disgustingly ugly. But tomorrow I shall be sober, and you will still be disgustingly ugly."

And this exchange with Nancy Astor who said, "If I was your wife I'd poison your coffee!" He replied, "If I was your husband I'd drink it."

Of Winston Churchill's epitaph: I am ready to meet my Maker. Whether my Maker is prepared for the great ordeal of meeting me is another matter.

Chapter 5: Winston's Life with Clementine

Clementine was tall, regal and willowy. She had a slapdash upbringing to be the wife of a Prime Minister, especially one that came from an aristocratic family. There was always some question about her true paternity. Her supposed father had never been interested in having children, and his "sexy, lonely, and bored" wife Lady Blanche looked elsewhere and in Clementine's case, to her brother in law, Lord Redesdale.

The Hoziers' hostile divorce, which seemed to mark Clementine's childhood, left Clementine's mother in dire straits financially. Even though Clementine had shown great promise academically, her mother pushed her out into society to attract a rich husband, instead of going to university.

Clementine's beauty did entice several suitors, but she broke off two engagements because her fiancés' were so dull. She was 22 when she met Winston Churchill, a young, rising politician, who was a son of a Duke. Winston Churchill was smitten right off the bat. He wrote her: "What a comfort and pleasure to meet a girl with so much intellectual quality." It was not long afterward that Winston proposed marriage to her at his family's home at Blenheim, and she was happy to accept. She scribbled him a note and sent it by one of Blenheim's footmen, "My Dearest One, I love you with all my heart and trust you."

For sixty years that trust and love stayed true. Clementine was Winston's adviser and confidante, scrutinizing his speeches, smoothing over his mistakes, and dealing with other politicians. She could dress down generals, command civil servants, face up to presidents on Winston's behalf, and tease cabinet members.

Even though she did not always agree with his political party; she always supported him in whatever decisions he made and defended him no matter what.

Clemmie was his support and his counselor when he again returned to lead the British government in the darker hours of World War II. Winston made Clemmie privy to top secret info, including the decrypts of the Nazi codes. She helped him run what some called "Operation Seduction U.S.A.", and that was to aid in getting the Americans to participate in the anti-Nazi struggle. She led Harry Hopkins on his visit to London so that he would promise help to Britain all the way to the end.

She forged a bond with Eleanor Roosevelt, even though the first lady had to wonder what was behind Clementine's public meekness to her husband, while the active Clementine was astounded by Mrs. Roosevelt's endless energy.

The Churchill's were known for their terrible fights. Winston would come out of a room closing the door behind him after they had a big, loud fight saying, "She called me a bloody old fool." But they were devoted to each other. Or should I say, Clementine was dedicated to Winston. Mary stated that "Father always came First, Second, and Third." By Clementine putting Winston first, she could conceal from the public the fact that he had a serious heart condition during World War II. When he started having strokes again, during his last time serving as prime minister, she hid that fact from the public as well.

When World War I broke out, Clementine was pregnant and alone. She had to take care of the children, and her mother, who suffered from what would now be called chronic fatigue syndrome. Clemmie appeared to have lost her mental well-being during this time, and eventually tried to hurt herself. When their 2-year-old daughter died, Clementine was a physical and emotional wreck. In 1963, she had to be hospitalized and go through shock therapy. When she would suffer from bouts of depression, she would go to bed, sometimes for a day or two. It seemed a defense mechanism against all the demands of her husband. I am sure it was no coincidence that after Winston Churchill died, that all her problems with her depression seemed to disappear.

It is sad to know that after Winston's death that Clementine had difficulty getting along financially and had to sell five of his paintings to be able to survive until her passing. When she died, she had only her one daughter, Mary Soames, and several grandchildren.

Chapter 6: The Day the Empire Ended

When Sir Winston Churchill died, it marked a grand finale in British history, that had been as magnificent as it was long.

Winston died on a Saturday morning, January 24, 1965, at his home in Hyde Park, London. He was 90 years old. Churchill suffered a massive stroke nine days earlier on January 15, 1965. It was exactly 70 years to the day since his father had died.

His death seemed historically significant. It came during a time when the Labour government was thinking about withdrawing all troops from the east of Suez, and that would close down the last of the British Empire. When Charles de Gaulle heard the news of Winston Churchill's death, he said, "Now Britain is no longer a great power."

The historian Sir Bryant wrote, "The day of giants is gone forever." Churchill's detective said, "If the king dies you can say 'Long live the king,' but now Sir Winston's gone, who is there? There is no one of his stature left." A. L. Rowse was just as pessimistic when he wrote: "The sun is going down on the British Empire."

When they found out about Churchill's death, the man who had responsibility for organizing his funeral, Earl Marshal, 16th Duke of Norfolk, began implementing the plans. The plan for Churchill's funeral was given the code name, "Operation Hope Not." When Churchill had suffered his stroke in 1953, meticulous arrangements had begun being made for his funeral.

The Queen had given instructions to Norfolk that Churchill's funeral should be befitting of his position in history". This would guarantee it would be the grandest state funeral for a commoner since the Duke of Wellington's funeral.

The arrangements for Churchill's funeral had to be continually updated because Churchill kept living and his pallbearers kept dying.

Churchill's main request for his funeral was that he wanted lots of military bands. He was to have nine.

January 30, 1965, millions of people around the world watched their televisions to see the largest state funeral that the world had ever seen. Big Ben's chimes echoed in the London silence. After the time was tolled at 9:45 a.m.; Winston Churchill lay under the bell. His flag-draped coffin rested on a gun carriage, as the terrible biting wind carried the loud roars of cannons that thundered a total of 90 shots, one for each year of the great Winston's life.

On command, there was a single drum that began to beat. Then you could hear the rhythmic pounding of boots upon the pavement as over 100 Royal Navy members moved in step as they drew the coffin of Churchill who had led Britain as Prime Minister during WWII and once again from 1951 to 1955. The nine military bands played songs, and somber marches as Winston's body continued to course through London streets escorted by servicemen from 20 various forces. Four majors from the Queen's Royal Irish Hussars carried Churchill's inventory of orders, medals, and decorations.

Churchill was the first civilian during the 20th century to attain the honor that was usually reserved for only queens and kings, and he was only the second Prime Minister given a State Funeral.

Winston lay in Westminster Hall (900 years old) as over 300,000 mourners passed by the casket that had been hewn from the English Oak trees taken from his family's estate. Even more people would have likely been there, had the temperature not dipped below zero. On the day of the funeral itself, it was so cold that even some of the police horses died from the cold. The Women's Volunteer Service and Salvation Army handed out sandwiches, tea, and soup, reminding those of the memories of wartime.

All across Britain, flags flew at half-mast. The newspapers were printing lengthy obituaries, black armbands were worn, sporting events rescheduled, shops closed that day, the schoolteacher's strike canceled. There was not going to be anything that would spoil this historic occasion.

At one point, there had been no less than 28 bombs from the war that had fallen on St. Paul's Cathedral. The church that had survived Hitler's attacks was the most obvious place to stage the funeral.

Before daylight on the day of the funeral, at least a million people lined the funeral route. They all watched in silence as the carriage rolled through the capital of Britain and routed past the offices where Churchill had served as the First Lord of the Admiralty. They traversed by the Fleet Street Newspaper, passing by 10 Downing Street from where he guided his country through some of its darkest times against the Nazis. Finally, the crowd moved past Trafalgar Square, where everyone gathered to celebrate when victory finally arrived at the end of the war, in 1945.

The procession lasted an hour, and its journey stopped at St. Paul's Cathedral. It was a lot like Churchill himself as it had become a symbol of Britain of the steely British determination as it managed to hold up during the worst of the Nazi bombing during the time of the Blitz.

The country had so much admiration for Winston that the Queen broke away from monarchical tradition and attended the funeral of someone that was not part of the royal family.

The Queen arrived at the cathedral before Churchill's casket had been delivered.

Inside St. Paul's, were dignitaries from 112 countries. That included six presidents, six monarchs, and 16 prime ministers; which made Winston's state funeral the biggest in history at that time. China refused to be involved, and Ireland did not broadcast the funeral. In addition to the 3,000 people that were at St. Paul's dome for the funeral, there were also about 350 million watching on television; there was a tenth of the entire world's population, looking at the funeral service. The television audience was larger than what it was for the funeral of President Kennedy that was held 15 months earlier. As the mourners sang "Battle Hymn of the Republic," there was a shaft of sunlight that broke through the clouds, and beamed directly through the cathedral's windows falling on the Union Jack that draped over Winston's casket.

After the service, Winston's coffin was then carried down the west steps of the cathedral. It was placed again on the carriage, which carried him on to a pier to the outside Tower of London, at which time the Royal Artillery fired a 19-gun salute.

As the procession passed the Cenotaph at Whitehall, men and women of the wartime resistance from Holland, Norway, Denmark, and France were carrying 100 flags and raised them in a final salute. After the passing of the coffin, Danish soldiers laid a wreath of lilies at the Cenotaph. A journalist asked for their names, and one of them responded by saying, "We were unknown at war, it must be the same now."

The funeral procession then boarded the Havengore for a short sail up the Thames. It was this part of the service that was methodically orchestrated for years, and perhaps the best remembered moment of the day was unscripted.

As 16 Royal Air Force fighter jets flew overhead in formation, it just happened that London's dockworkers dipped their cranes one by one, as if the massive machines were bowing their heads to Winston.

When the Havengore finally docked, Churchill's casket was taken to Waterloo Station. It was placed on a train that was specially fitted with five Pullman coaches prepared for family and friends of Churchill's final Journey, to his resting place.

The train chugged the 60-miles to Oxfordshire, while mourners on station platforms stood with bowed heads and hats over their hearts, along with World War II vets in uniforms saluting.

Then, not far from Blenheim Palace where Churchill was born 90 years before, his life had come full circle. During a private ceremony in a quiet churchyard located in the village of Bladon, Winston's body was then lowered into the small family plot and covered over with the very soil that he had worked so hard to preserve to stay British.

The ceremony left De Gaulle impressed. He spoke with genuine feeling about how well Earl Marshal had organized the monumental event.

Clementine, in everyone's opinion, "carried herself like a queen." When she went to bed after a terribly exhausting and emotional day, she told Mary, her daughter: "It was not a funeral, it was a triumph!"

Montague Browne, the last private secretary to work for Churchill, was invited to mourn with the family. He said, "black melancholy thoughts of the decline and decay of so much of what Churchill had stood for. Well, might the nation mourn him."

And if that was not bad enough, for the fact that Montague was mourning for his boss, highlighting the fact of the British moral decay, when Montague got back to his flat in London, he realized he had been robbed.

I do not believe that there was one person that Winston Churchill ever met, that he failed to inspire or impress. One has to wonder, what would have changed in the course of history, if Hitler would have dined with the Churchill Family. We will always have the possibilities to ponder.

Conclusion

Thanks again for taking the time to read this book!

You should now have a good understanding of Winston Churchill and his fascinating life!

If you enjoyed this book, please take the time to leave me a review on Amazon. I appreciate your honest feedback, and it really helps me to continue producing high quality books.

www.ingramcontent.com/pod-product-compliance
Lightning Source LLC
LaVergne TN
LVHW021207140726
843272LV00042B/1225